# Testimonials

Ron Lever's ethical will is a wonderful model for us all. Blending serious moral discussions with personal anecdotes, he has shown us all how to leave a living legacy which will spark the interest and shape the souls of our children and grandchildren.
**Elliot Dorff, Rector and Distinguished Professor of Philosophy, University of Judaism**

As a mother of eight, I have been inspired to put into writing my family history and pass onto my children the Christian values and lessons which I have learned in life. Your work is truly inspiring and inspired.
**Gloria Macklin, Los Angeles**

Thank you for sharing your ethical will book with me. It is a gift that your grandchildren will always treasure.
**Rabbi Jack Riemer, Author, So Your Values Live On, Ethical Wills and How to Prepare Them.**

You have done an important thing. I am greatly honored by your kind references to my work.
**Dennis Praeger, Author and Talk Show Host**

Ron Lever has, with loving thoughtfulness, gathered together intuitions, learning and aspirations that serve as a moral legacy. It is a book of inspiration.
**Rabbi Harold M. Schulweis, Valley Beth Shalom**

A love letter filled with good humor and good advice. It offers a wonderful model for anyone who wishes to prepare the same gift for their family.
**Dr. Ron Wolfson, Vice President, University of Judaism. Author, The Art of Jewish Living Series.**

Ron Lever's work brings to mind the recent film *My Big Fat Greek Wedding*, which depicts a lifestyle resonant in other cultures. As a Catholic, I could feel many common themes. It is a spiritual interreligious family experience.
**Reverend Monsignor Royale M. Vadakin**

This type of material is much needed by today's youth, who are not being taught values and ethics for fear of making them feel unworthy. It has great photos and quotations.
**Arline Chase, Author and Writing Coach**

How lucky are those children who can share the wisdom and legacy of their grandparents. How lucky are we to join Ron Lever on his journey and partake in his deep reflections.
**Rabbi Ed Feinstein, Valley Beth Shalom**

Your book is moving and inspiring. The worksheet is an excellent way to focus attention on what we want to say to our own children in our ethical wills.
**Fleurette Hershman, Los Angeles**

A loving book which talks about ethical values in language that children can understand. Each lesson is presented through stories from grandpa's or grandchild's experience. Use this book as a model for your own cherished legacy.
**Sylvia Weishaus, PhD., Marriage and Family Therapist**

Thank you for sharing your ethical will with me. I know it will be treasured by your family for generations. It is an exemplary example of putting ones thoughts and values together and writing them down.
**Rabbi Harold S. Kushner, Author, When Bad Things Happen to Good People.**

# An
# Ethical Will

# Grandpa Teaches Values

## Ron Lever

## (Ronnie, Daddy, Doctor Lever, Uncle Ronnie and Grandpa)

ISBN 0-9723446-9-1
LCCN: 2002095745

# Dedications

*To my wife Doreen*
    You are the wind beneath my wing.
    I'm so fortunate you chose to share your life with me.


*To my children Karen and Rick*
    You are my window into the future.
    I'm very proud of your accomplishments.


*To my grandchildren Rubin, Shifra, Jeremie and Ilana*
    I see the future through your eyes.
    I wish I could always be there for you.


*To my friends*
    You know who you are.
    We owe everything to each other.
    No thanks are adequate.


*To my teacher*
    You teach with a gentle soul.
    My writing continues to improve.


*To my writer classmates*
    Your comments are invaluable.
    You never let me off the hook.


*To my readers*
    Thank you for sharing my labor of love.
    I pray to touch you in some small way.

Anyone who teaches his grandchildren,
It is deemed as if he had personally,
Received the Torah at Mount Sinai.
Talmud, Kedushin 30b

You shall make them known unto thy
children, And thy children's children

Deuteronomy 4:9

Grandpa 1½ Yrs.
Cover Grandpa 4½ Yrs.

**Grandpa's Mother and Father**
**At their wedding, September 2, 1923.**
**Morris Lever, age 25.  Anna Wyloge, age 19.**

# Table of Contents

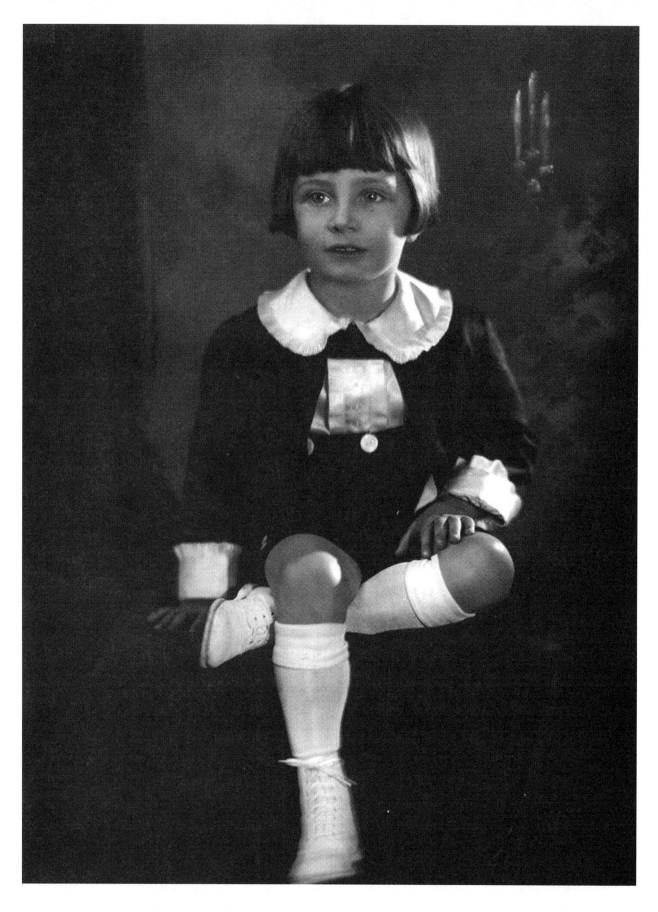

**Grandpa's brother Stanley at 4 years in 1928
at the wedding of Uncle Nathan and Aunt Sophie.
He has a Buster Brown haircut and suit.**

# Introduction

I went to my synagogue, Valley Beth Shalom in Encino, California. Rabbi Harold Schulweis was giving us an important message. He said:

- "Write your Ethical Will.
- Leave it for your children and grandchildren.
- Tell them the moral values you have learned to live by."

I thought that this was a great idea. And I soon forgot about it.

I went back the next week. Rabbi Ed Feinstein was delivering his usual brilliant sermon. He said:

- "A lot of things have happened to you over the years.
- You have gained your wisdom the hard way.
- Write it down."

The Rabbi was right. I had something important to say, and so I began to write it down. The result is *An Ethical Will,* subtitled *Grandpa Teaches Values.*

Ethical wills are a longtime Jewish tradition which could also enrich other cultures. The first recorded one was written by Moses as the "Book of Deuteronomy" in the *Torah.* Jack Riemer and Nathaniel Stampfer have compiled many of them in their book, *So That Your Values Live On, Ethical Wills and How to Prepare Them.* It tells how Jewish people have passed along their values from one generation to another.

It is difficult to write any kind of will. Writing this book has forced me to face my own mortality and wonder when the end will come; however, no one is permitted to know the exact time and circumstances of his or her death. I would like to live to be one hundred and twenty, like Moses. His mind was clear and he was mentally and physically vigorous to the end. In the meantime, I plan to take the advice of Kohelet in the *Book of Ecclesiastes* and enjoy each day to the fullest.

My fondest wish is that I can inspire you to write your own Ethical Will. Perhaps you could make it a family project. Start by looking at pictures of your children or grandchildren. Write them a letter and tell them what you think is important. Take it a step further and read it to them. Have a discussion. You might be encouraged to expand your letter into an essay or even into a book, as I did. It will be one of the most rewarding experiences you will ever have. Your heirs will be grateful, and they will treasure it forever.

To help you get started, I have prepared a worksheet on pages 83 and 84. Make a copy of these pages and fill them out as soon as possible. I hope it will inspire you to do more. If you don't do anything further, it will be enough.

Jewish values have been summed up by the Hebrew words:

- Torah  (Study)
- Mitzvot  (Observation of the commandments)
- G'Milut Chasadim  (Acts of loving kindness)

The great sage, Hillel, was once asked to sum up Judaism while standing on one foot. He replied, "What is hateful to you, do not do to your neighbor. The rest is commentary. Now go and study."

That is the Golden Rule. If you don't read any further, I would like to leave you with this important message.

## Yom Kippur Prayer

Birth is a beginning,

And death is a destination.

Life is a journey,

A sacred pilgrimage,

To life everlasting.

## Ecclesiastes 2:24

There is nothing better for a man,

That he should eat and drink,

And that he should make his soul,

Take pleasure in his labor.

**Grandpa's Mother Anna with her brothers and sisters.
Left to right: Uncle Herman, Mother Anna, Aunt Rose,
Uncle Sam, Aunt Ettie, Aunt Sadie, and Uncle Moishe.**

## Things to Think About

1. Have you heard about Ethical Wills before?
2. Do you think it would be a good idea for you to write one?
3. Are values as important as money?
4. Do you think your children and grandchildren would treasure your Ethical Will?
5. Would you enjoy reading it out loud with them?
6. Should only Jews write Ethical Wills?
7. Would you like to write one? Start now. Turn to page 83.

## Things to Write About

1. What values are important to me?
2. What ethical values would I like to teach my children and grandchildren?
3. What special hopes do I have for them?
4. What warnings do I want to give them?
5. What other personal messages would I like to write to them?

# Chapter 1

## Even Grandpas Make Mistakes

We were sitting around the table and talking. I began to tell a story.

"Last year when we were in Jerusalem..."

Ilana says, "Grandpa, it was two years ago that you were in Israel."

"You are right. You know..."

Rubin, Shifra, Jeremie and Ilana all laugh and say, "We know. Even grandpas make mistakes. That's what you always say."

"You are right," I respond. "I am only human. I'm entitled to make mistakes, just like everyone else."

Rubin says, "Why don't you just deny making the mistake. Nobody will know the difference most of the time."

"I don't have to deny it. There is no need for me to pretend to be perfect. Moses was not perfect. He stuttered so badly that he asked his brother Aaron to speak to the Pharoah for him."

"God is perfect," Jeremie states.

"God also makes mistakes," I explain.

"Where did you hear that?"

"I read it in the Bible. It says in Genesis that God created man and woman. Within a few generations people started to misbehave. So, He decided to destroy them all in a flood and start all over again with Noah and his family."

Jeremie says, "One mistake is not so bad."

"I can think of two more times that God showed that He wasn't perfect. After the Golden Calf incident, He was going to destroy all of our people and start all over again. Moses talked him out of it. Then there was the time that Abraham argued with God about destroying all of the people in Sodom and Gemorrah."

Ilana says, "My teacher tells me that everybody makes mistakes. That is why they put erasers on pencils."

"Yes. I agree with her and I can give you some examples from sports:

- Good quarterbacks only complete one half of all the passes they throw.

- The best basketball players only make one basket for every two shots they take.

- Babe Ruth struck out more times than he hit home runs."

Jeremie says, "Maybe we should give up and not try."

"No, we can't use that as an excuse. We still have to try to do our best. We just have to be realistic and realize that sometimes we fall short of our expectations."

"I know someone who thinks he is always right," Rubin says. "Adam, in my class gets upset if you tell him he did anything wrong."

"That's too bad," I explain, "because I learn a lot from my mistakes. First, I try to figure out what I did wrong. Then I try to not make the same mistake again."

Rubin shakes his head up and down, "I think you are right. He does the same dumb things over and over again."

"It's too much trouble to pretend to be perfect all the time. It's too big a burden to carry. The best thing to do is to admit the mistake right away. I usually say, 'You are right,' or

'Thank you for pointing that out.' It saves a lot of time. I want to use my time to enjoy the better things in life."

## Ecclesiastes 7:20

For there is not one righteous man on earth.
Who is always good, and has never sinned.

## Joel 3:1

Your old shall dream dreams,
And your young shall see visions.

**Grandma's Father, Joe Calof and Family in 1918**
**Bottom row, left to right: Grandma's Grandfather, John Calof,**
**Uncles Morrie and Sam Calof, and Grandmother Sarah.**
**Top row, left to right: Grandma's Uncle Roy and father Joe Calof.**

## Things to think about

1. Have you ever made a mistake?
2. Do you hate to admit you made an error?
3. Are other people happy to point out your mistakes?
4. Is there anyone who is perfect all the time in everything?
5. What is the worst thing that can happen if you admit you made a mistake?
6. Do others really care about your mistakes?
7. Can you ever cover up a mistake?
8. Will the truth eventually be revealed?
9. Why try to do your best if you make mistakes?
10. Can you learn from your mistakes and become a better person?

## Things to write about

1. Describe some of the mistakes you have made.
2. Did you admit them or cover them up?
3. How you learned from your mistakes?
4. Do you know people who never admit to making mistakes?

# Chapter 2
## Apologize and Forgive

It was during Rosh Hashanah several years ago. I don't remember the exact date. I was sitting in my usual seat at Valley Beth Shalom in Encino, California. Doreen was singing in the choir as she usually does. Rabbi Schulweis was giving a sermon. I was only half listening. My attention returned when he said, "This is a new year. It is a time for new beginnings. What you didn't like about your life last year, you can change in this coming year. It is your opportunity to start your life all over again."

I was now completely focused on his message. He continued. "We come to synagogue to make our peace with God. That is the easy part. We also have to make our peace with people we have hurt along the way." He reminded us about various ways we hurt others. We do it:

- intentionally and unintentionally
- knowingly and unknowingly
- by things we say and by things we don't say
- by things we do or don't do

"According to our tradition," he said, "You have to apologize to those you may have hurt and ask for their forgiveness. You also need to genuinely forgive them for any harm they may have done to you."

I looked around and saw Doctor Sam Goldwyn sitting a few rows away from me in his customary seat. He saw me and looked right through me. We hadn't spoken for years. The original cause of the problem happened so long ago that I couldn't even remember it. I wondered if he did.

Should I apologize to Sam? Will he accept my apology or will he reject me? Will he think I'm crazy? In the spirit of the holiday I decided to give it a try. During the break, I hesitated a little bit, then I walked up to him. As I approached he gave me a look that seemed to ask, "What in the world are you up to now?"

I said, "Sam, I want to apologize for what I did to upset you and hope you will forgive me."

He was silent for a moment. He looked into my eyes and studied me. Finally he said, "I appreciate what you are trying to do. I'm glad you came over." He shook my hand and said, "Let's get together and talk some more."

We never had that talk, but became friends.

I was motivated by this episode and went on to make my peace with everyone I could. The outcome has always been successful. I have been much happier since then.

We all have made our enemies along the way. I highly recommend making amends with them. Like me, you will be pleased with the results. It frees you and the other person from the poisonous emotion of hatred. There may also be some feeling of guilt on both sides. It is best to cast everything aside with mutual forgiveness. Then each person can go on with his or her life in a more positive manner, with less baggage to carry because hatred or resentment is a heavy load.

To each and every one of you, I humbly apologize for anything that I may have said or done to hurt you. I appeal for your forgiveness. Pardon me for your own sake, as well as for mine. I also forgive you for any harm you may have caused me. I don't want you to be burdened any longer by any negative feelings because of me. Toss them out and don't let them hamper your life in any way.

## The Merchant of Venice Act 1, Sc.1

The quality of mercy is not strained,

It dropeth as the gentle rain from heaven.

Upon the place beneath,

It is twice blest.

It blesseth him that gives and him that takes.

**Shakespeare**

## The Merchant of Venice Act III, Sc. 1
### Shylock

I am a Jew, hath not a Jew eyes?

If you prick us, do we not bleed?

If you tickle us, do we not laugh?

If you poison us, do we not die.

**Shakespeare**

## Things to think about

1. Are there some people you are not talking to because you are mad at them?
2. Can you remember the cause of the problem?
3. Are you entirely right? Are they entirely wrong?
4. How does it make you feel when you come in contact with someone who doesn't like you?
5. Do you look at him or her? How does he or she look at you?
6. How many members of your family are not talking to one another?
7. Do you have the courage to make up with people who don't like you?
8. What is the worst that could happen if you fail?
9. Would it hurt to apologize, even if you are right?
10. Would you lead a happier life if every person on this earth liked you?


## Things to write about

1. The people I have offended.
2. The people who have offended me.
3. The people I have made up with.
4. The happiness that results from getting along with people.

# Chapter 3

## You Are Already Rich

There are many restaurants on Ventura Boulevard near our house. We often walk to them. Our grandchildren's favorite is *Johnny Rockets*, a hamburger place decorated in the fifties style. It has a nickel jukebox that plays old songs. The hamburgers are juicy and come with fried onions. Along the walk, we get to talk.

They say, "Grandpa, when we grow up, we want to be rich."

I say to them, "You are already rich. You live in a nice house. You each have your own bedroom. You have lots of toys. What more could you want?"

"Yeah, but all of our friends have that."

I want to tell them that money doesn't buy happiness. I start to say, "When I was a boy..."

They all say at the same time, "Yes we know, Grandpa. There was no television. All you had was a radio. You had to walk two miles to school, barefoot in the snow." I try a different approach.

"Let me tell you a story I heard from Dennis Prager on the radio.

They hadn't heard this one, so they all say "OK Let's hear it."

There was a man who wanted to be on the list of the five hundred richest people in America. He struggled and sacrificed everything he had. He also lost his family and friends along the way. Then one day he opened the newspaper: There was his name on the list. He was number five hundred."

Rubin says, "Then he was happy, right?"

"Yes, but only for a short time. He became unhappy again when he realized that there were so many people ahead of him on the list."

"Then what did he do?" Jeremie asks.

"He renewed his struggle and worked night and day, including weekends and holidays. By perseverance and luck he was able to reach number one."

"That's a good story. I'll bet he was really happy," says Shifra.

"That's not the end of it. He became even more unhappy when he realized that there were so many people who wanted to replace him at the top. He had to work harder than ever just to stay where he was."

Jeremie says, "What a bummer. Are you telling us that it's better not to have anything?"

"No, there is no virtue in being poor. You need to work hard to earn a good living for yourself and your family."

Shifra says, "That doesn't make sense. How can you work hard and still enjoy life?"

"It's not easy. You just have to keep both objectives in mind and try to achieve a balance. This dilemma is one of the many challenges that makes life worthwhile."

"Not only that, the Bible says we have to give ten percent of our income to people who are less fortunate than we are. It is called *Tzadakah*, which means justice. It is not called charity. Even people who are on welfare have to give to people who are poorer than they are."

"Yeah. We learned that in Sunday School," says Ilana.

I continue, "Remember when we went to the Children's Zoo? There was a plaque with the names of people who donated money. I pointed out that there were a lot of Jewish names on the list. In our heritage we have a strong commitment to give something back to the community."

Rubin asks, "Are you saying that only Jews donate money to good causes?"

"No, of course not. Some people donate and some do not. I always admire those who give generously of their time and money."

Jeremie asks, "Where did you learn about that?"

"When we get back home, I will show you a small book called *Pirke Avot*, also known as *The Wisdom of the Fathers*. It is full of inspirational sayings that I like to read from time to time. It is part of the Talmud written by the ancient Rabbis who shaped the form of Judaism that we practice today. It asks the question, "Who is rich?" It goes on to answer, "He who is content with his portion (what he has)."

I tell them, "You are already rich. You love each other. You have everything you need. What more could you want?"

They smile and say, "Grandpa, we mean really rich."

### Pirke Avot (Wisdom of the Fathers) 4:2

Who is wise?  He who learns from every man.

Who is strong?  He who conquers his passions.

Who is rich?  He who is content with what he has.

Who is honored?  He who honors others.

# Things to think about

1. Are people rich because they have a lot of money?
2. How much money do you need to consider yourself rich?
3. Are most rich people satisfied with what they have?
4. Why do so many rich people want to make more and more money?
5. Why don't some poor children realize they are poor?
6. Can you be satisfied with what you already have?
7. Do family and friends make a person rich?
8. Would you be rich with a bigger or better car or a bigger house?
9. Can you tell the difference between what you need and what you want?
10. Is your neighbor's grass really greener than yours?

# Things to write about

1. Am I rich or poor?
2. How much money will it take to make me rich?
3. Will I be satisfied when I have that amount?
4. Am I willing to work harder to become rich?
5. Does money buy happiness?
6. Does money rent happiness for a while?

# Spector Family - 50th Anniversary - 1942

Grandma Doreen, age 11, front row center.
Her Grandparents, Morris and Bessie Spector are behind her.
Her father, Joe Calof, third row extreme right.
Her mother, Edith Spector, second row, extreme right.

Front Row      Ronnie Zane, Rhoda Lee Zane, Doreen Calof, Arlene Spector, David Minkoff, Harriet Spector.

Second Row    Rose Mitnick, Ethel Stall, Bessie Spector, Morris Spector, Sarah Mittleman, Max Spector, Fannie Spector, Edith Calof.

Third Row      Chana Gitel Needleman, Rose Spector, Della Spector, Leonard Spector, Selma Levy, Charles Levy, Alexander Zane, Clara Zane, Art Minkoff, Esther Minkoff, Louie Spector, Ruth Spector, Sybil Calof, Zivee Calof, Joe Calof.

# The Lever House in City Terrace, CA. - 1945

Some of the family came to see my brother Stanley when he
was discharged from the army.  He took the picture and is not in it.

Front Row:      Uncle Danny, Aunt Sadie and Cousin Roberta Schwartz, Cousins
                 Ethyl and Allen Gardner.
Second Row:  Baba (Grandmother) Lena Wyloge, Aunt Ettie Gardner, Zayda
                 (Grandfather) Kalman Wyloge, Aunt Edith and Cousin Rivee
                 Belenzon, Mother Anna and Father Morris Lever.
Third Row:     Cousin Audrey and Aunt Rose Greenberg, Uncle Moishe Wyloge,
                 Uncle Max Belenzon, That's me, Ronnie Lever, Cousin Ronnie (Bab
                 Greenberg, Cousin Artie Belenzon.
Back Row:      Uncle Mickey Greenberg, Uncle Henry Gardner.

# Chapter 4

## Does God Exist?

Shifra asks, "Grandpa, have you ever seen God?"

"Yes." I tell her, "I see the face of God whenever I look at you." I know she is asking me about the existence of God. I wrestle with this problem, just like every other thinking person. Rabbis' say that it takes a leap of faith. They have told me that they also have their doubts from time to time. The only people who have no doubts are the orthodox believers of all faiths. They accept everything unquestioningly. I am not as fortunate as they are and have to struggle with the question about the existence of God.

She goes on, "Our teacher says that we are all made in the image of God. Does that mean that He looks like us?"

"We don't really know what God looks like. I'm sure that He does not have arms and legs and a white beard and talk with a deep voice like Charlton Heston."

"Who is Charlton Heston?"

"He is the actor who played Moses in the movie, "The Ten Commandments." A lot of people think that God looks like him. As a matter of fact we really shouldn't use the word He because God is not a man or a woman."

"Everyone looks different. How can we all be born in God's image?"

"Yes, everyone is different. Yet they all have a spark of God in them. Everyone deserves to be treated with respect. Each of us has a special talent and we each have something to contribute. This is the Jewish concept of *Tikun Olam,* which states that everyone has a part to play in making this world a better place."

"Why do we need God? Everyone knows what is right and what is wrong."

"Without God everything would just be a matter of opinion. You would do something that you think is right and Rebecca would think that it was wrong. That's what we call *Relativism*. Right and wrong is relative to each person's point of view."

"As a matter of fact, I remember when I needed a pen and I borrowed hers without telling her," Shifra says. "She got mad and said that I stole it. I was going to give it back."

"That is what I mean. God gives us values that apply to everyone. We have the Ten Commandments and other moral laws that we all have to obey."

"Why can't we just do what's right for the people of the world? We can make our own laws."

"That is what we call *Humanism*. It means that people make up their own morals. It has been tried and it doesn't work. Adolph Hitler, who was the dictator of Germany during World War II, made terrible laws. He thought that they were for the good of the German people. He was wrong. A system called *Communism* was popular for a while. It said that everyone takes what he needs and gives what he can."

"That sounds good. I'll bet it works."

"It was a disaster. Everyone wanted to take and nobody wanted to give."

"Did you always believe in God?"

"No, I used to be a firm believer in the religion of *Science*. There was no doubt in my mind that sooner or later science would come up with all of the answers. We would have no need for God. The only problem is that every scientific discovery leads to more questions. We do experiments and figure out what happens, but we can't figure out why they happen."

"Can't we get all the answers if we just study hard enough?"

"The more I study, the more I find that Science and Religion are drawing closer together. The most popular theory of the origin of the universe is the *Big Bang Theory*. It states that the universe started with a big bang. But, it doesn't tell us who or what caused the big bang in the first place."

I see her staring at me. I say, "What is wrong? Why are you looking at me like that?"

"I can see the face of God in you too, Grandpa."

## Malachi 2:10

Have we not all one father?

Did not one God create us all?

Why do we deal treacherously with one another,

profaning the covenant of our fathers?

## Job 31:15

Did not he that made me,

in my mother's womb,

make him.

# Things to think about

1. Does God really exist?
2. Is God Christian, Moslem, Hindu, Buddhist, Jewish, etc?
3. Why doesn't God show himself or herself to us?
4. Why does he or she let children and other innocent people suffer and die?
5. Can you be good without God?
6. Is goodness relative to each person's point of view?
7. Why does God allow good people to suffer and bad people to prosper?
8. Does God always punish us when we are bad and reward us when we are good?
9. Will he or she reward us in the afterlife?
10. Will God reward us when the Messiah comes or returns?
11. Has the Holocaust destroyed your faith in God?

# Things to write about

1. What are your ideas about God?
2. What do other people think about God?
3. Is there room in this world for different beliefs?
4. What qualities do you see in people that remind you of God?

# Chapter 5

# Happiness

One night, after a Passover Seder, we are sitting at the table and talking. I ask my grandchildren, "What would you like to be?"

Jeremie says, "I want to go into business and make a lot of money."

Ilana says, "I want to be a movie star. I want to be rich and famous."

Rubin says, "I want to have lots of fun."

Shifra doesn't answer right away. She is deep in thought. We all look at her. Finally, she states, "I don't care about any of that stuff. I just want to be happy."

Ilana says, "Me too."

Jeremie says, "You're right. That is the most important thing."

Rubin says, "That's what I mean. You're happy when you're having fun."

I explain, "You know Rubin, I have learned that having fun and happiness are not the same thing."

"What do you mean?" he asks.

"I see pictures of movie stars and rock singers in the magazines all the time. They seem to be having fun and enjoying themselves."

"That's exactly what I mean," he remarks.

I say, "Later on, a lot of them write books and tell about how unhappy they really were. Some of them get hooked on drugs, and some of them even try to commit suicide."

"What do they have to be unhappy about?" He asks, "They have everything they want. They have all of the money they need. They have lots of friends. They have cars and clothes and can buy anything they want."

"They find out that it takes more than fun to be happy. They have a little fun, and then they want more. Then they want more and more. Believe it or not, they get bored, having all that fun. They want to know what it takes to be happy."

"What does it take?" asks Shifra.

"I read a book by Dennis Prager called *Happiness is a Serious Problem.*"

"Does he tell us how to be happy?" asks Jeremie.

"He says that happiness is not a goal. It is a journey. You become happy when you work toward something that is worthwhile."

Rubin says, "I'm lost. You'll have to translate that for me."

I ask him, "You're happy playing on the freshman football team, correct? But, I'll bet it's not fun all the time. Is it?"

"You bet it's not. I get home after five o'clock every day and I'm tired. I have to do my homework and eat and go to sleep. Then I have to get up at six thirty and start all over again."

"See what I mean?"

"Yeah, but I can't play football all my life. What is a good goal for me?"

"Dennis Prager doesn't tell us that, and I can't tell you either. Everyone is different. He says that you just have to find it out for yourself. Your goal has to be something that gives your life meaning. From that you gain a feeling of inner peace and self-respect. That is what leads to happiness."

Rubin says, "I think he is right. My dad is happy and he works very hard."

"I think you have hit the nail right on the head. What do you think is his goal?"

Shifra explains, "He spends a lot of time with us. I think that he wants us to be a good family."

I agree, "Yes and he is doing an excellent job. Your grandmother and I are very proud of him."

I continue, "From personal experience, I can also tell you that happiness almost always involves being with other people. There are times you need to be alone, but these are usually not the happy times in life. I have found the most happiness while I was trying to make others happy."

Rubin says, "I remember when I gave Ilana a book that she really wanted. I saw her face light up with a smile that was worth a lot more than what I paid for the book."

He continues, "I know someone who is very selfish. I won't mention his name, but all he talks about is himself. He doesn't care about anyone else."

"I'll bet he is unhappy and makes everyone else around him unhappy," I reply.

"That's exactly what happens," Rubin says. "He's a real downer."

I go on to tell them, "I have also found that happiness can't be forced. The worst time I ever had was at a New Year's Eve party. There were noisemakers and funny hats and champagne. Everyone was supposed to have fun drinking and yelling 'Happy New Year'. I found myself watching the clock and waiting to leave. The happiest times I have had were with family and friends when we were talking and enjoying each other's company."

## Song Kicks

Don't it seem like,

Kicks just keep getting harder to find.

And all your kicks,

Ain't bringing you peace of mind.

Before you find out it's too late,

You better get straight.

**Paul Revere and the Raiders**

## Isaiah 2:4

They shall beat their swords into plowshares,

And their spears into pruning hooks.

Nation shall not lift up sword against nation,

And they shall never again know war.

## Things to think about

1. How many people do you know who are really happy?
2. Is fun the same thing as happiness?
3. Can you have so much fun that you get bored?
4. Will you be happy when you achieve your goals?
5. Why don't drugs and alcohol lead to happiness?
6. Can an unhappy person transform himself into a happy person?
7. What does it take to start being happy?
8. Can a happy person be unhappy at times?
9. What does it mean that happiness is in the journey and not the goal?
10. Are you happy alone or only when you are with other people?

## Things to write about

1. The happy times in my life.
2. The unhappy times in my life.
3. What I have learned about happiness.
4. What advice I can give about happiness.

**Grandpa's Aunt Sophie and Uncle Harry**

**Grandma's mother and father
Edith and Joe Calof**

**Grandpa's Father, Morris, top left
Uncle Nathan, bottom right**

**Grandma as a baby
Her mother Edith Calof**

# Chapter 6

## That's Not Fair

My son Rick makes some popcorn. He puts a movie he rented in the VCR. He and the kids start to watch. Suddenly his beeper goes off. There is an emergency at the hospital. He has to go. Rubin, who is 14, has to baby-sit the younger ones, and they all have to stay home.

"That's not fair," says Rubin. "I wanted to go rollerblading with Joseph."

"That's not fair," says Shifra. "I wanted to go over to Sarah's to play."

"That's not fair," says Jeremie. "You said you would take me shopping."

"That's not fair," says Ilana. "Why do you always have to work?"

Rick becomes exasperated and says, "Life is not fair."

They all start to talk at once.

Rick regains his composure and tells them, "When I come home we'll go to the mall and see a movie." They are still not satisfied and continue to say, "That's not fair."

He says to them, "How come you guys always tell me that I'm not fair?"

"Well, Dad, you taught us to be fair," Jeremie replies.

"You know I have to work. Why do you have to give me a hard time? You have to be fair to me, too."

Shifra says, "I never thought about it like that. What we think is fair can be unfair to you."

Dad says, "That's right. You need to see things from my point of view."

Rubin says, "We want to be fair. We learned in Sunday School that good people get rewarded and bad people get punished."

Dad says, "Generally that's what happens. Unfortunately there are times when people cheat and win and other's play by the rules and lose."

Jeremie says, "That's really unfair."

Dad says, "I really think that in the long run cheaters never prosper."

"What's prosper?" asks Ilana.

"I mean that sooner or later cheaters get caught and lose everything they have won. People who play by the rules eventually win."

"Why doesn't it happen right away?" says Shifra.

Dad laughs, "I knew you would ask me that. It is a really tough question. Sometimes you have to wait a while for justice to be done."

Jeremie says, "How long do you have to wait?"

"Usually it doesn't take too long. Some people say you may have to wait to get your rewards in the next world. Others say that we may have to wait until the Messiah comes."

Rubin asks, "Dad, why does God allow bad things to happen to good people?"

"I don't know. I asked Grandpa the same question when I was your age and he said that he didn't know either. He said that people have wondered about it for thousands of years. He told me how Job in the Bible asked God why he was being treated unfairly. God spoke to Job from a whirlwind. He did not give Job a good answer, but Job was satisfied that God took the time to talk to him."

Shifra says, "Our teacher lost her whole family in the Holocaust. She has lost faith in fairness."

"She is right. The Holocaust is the best example of evil in the world. Hitler and the Nazis were defeated and they got their well-deserved punishment."

"Yes, but not until millions of innocent people were killed." says Shifra.

"I wish I could tell you why God let it happen. Grandpa and Grandma took your Aunt Karen and me to Israel when we were teenagers. We visited Yad Vashem, which is a memorial to the six million Jews killed by the Nazis in World War II. We saw pictures of smiling, innocent children. One and one half million of them were killed. Grandpa gets tears in his eyes when he talks about it."

"Maybe we should just give up," says Shifra.

"No, that's not the answer. You still have to try to do what is right. Grandpa says that the Messiah will come when everyone is doing his or her share to make this world a better place in which to live."

## Ecclesiastes 7:14,15
In the time of prosperity be joyful.

And in the time of adversity, reflect.

God gives one as well as the other.

So that we may realize that nothing is certain.

In this life, I have seen both of these:

A good man perishes in spite of his goodness,
And a wicked man lives on in his wickedness.

## Things to think about

1. Is life always fair? Why not?
2. How do you tell children that things are not always fair?
3. How do you teach children to be fair to others?
4. Is it fair when bad things happen to good people?
5. Is it fair for good things to happen to bad people?
6. Why do children have to suffer and die?
7. Do we get what's coming to us in life?
8. Do we get our rewards in the afterlife?
9. Do we have to wait for the Messiah in order to get fairness?
10. Should you give up your faith in fairness?

## Things to write about

1. The unfair things that have happened to you.
2. The unfair things you have seen.
3. Why is there unfairness in life?
4. What I can do about it.

**Grandpa - 2 years**
**Cousin Babe Greenberg - 1½**

**13 years later**

# 1944

clockwise
from top left

Mother Anna
and Ron.

Father Morris
and Ron.

Uncle Danny,
Cousin Roberta,
Aunt Sadie, and
Zayda Kalman.

Ron, Mother
Anna, Brother
Stanley, and
Father Morris.

# Chapter 7

# Generosity Pays

It is Ilana's seventh birthday party. She is excited and has not eaten her cake.

Jeremie, who is eleven asks, "Can I have your cake?"

"No," she answers, as she moves her plate away and shields it with her arm.

"Why don't you share your cake with Jeremie?" Grandma asks, "You are not going to eat it anyway."

"No, it's mine and he can't have it."

I think that I might be able to solve this problem with a few words of wisdom. I say, "Let me tell you about something I read in The Book of Ecclesiastes."

Their focus moves from the cake to me and they turn to listen.

"Kohelet, the priest, was a very wise man, like King Solomon. He tells us, 'Cast your bread upon the waters and it will return to you. Give to many for you, yourself, may need much help in the days ahead.'"

"What does that mean?" Jeremie and Ilana ask at the same time.

"He is saying that the more you give away, the more you get in return."

Jeremie says, "I understand that part, but what about giving to many?"

"He is telling us to spread it around. Be generous to a lot of people. You never know when you may need help in the future."

"That makes sense," he says.

I had barely finished talking when Ilana looks over at Jeremie's plate. Even though she had not eaten her cake, she says, "That's not fair. He got two scoops of ice cream and I only got one. I want some more."

Grandma goes to the freezer. "The ice cream is all gone. Maybe Jeremie will share some of his with you."

Jeremie moves his plate away. "No," he says. "I got it first. It's mine."

Grandma tells him, "If you are generous and share your ice cream with Ilana, then she will be generous and share her cake with you. If you are selfish and don't share with her, she will be selfish and won't share with you."

"I don't care," he says.

I think maybe I should try again. "Let me tell you about Job, which is my favorite book in the Bible."

"OK," they say. "We'll listen. Tell us another story."

"Job was a very good man who was also very rich. Satan looked at him and was jealous. He talked God into letting him test Job. He bet that Job would not be so good if he were not so rich. Satan then proceeded to take away everything Job had and made him even more miserable with boils all over his body."

"Yuck," says Ilana. "I wouldn't want to be him. What happened next?"

"He was not bitter as you might expect. He said, 'God gives and God takes back. I came into this world naked and I'm going to leave it the same way.'"

"What does that mean?" asks Jeremie.

"No matter how rich you are, you can't take your money with you when you die."

Jeremie says, "I'm too young to die, but I am going to make a lot of money."

"From your mouth to God's ear," I say. "Job is also telling us that we don't really own anything. Everything we have, including our own body is on loan to us from God. He expects us to enjoy everything we have for the time we have it. But, we have to give it all back in the end. It doesn't make sense to hoard things and keep them all to ourselves."

Jeremie says, "I'm going to be very generous and give to a lot of charities. Ilana you can have some of my ice cream."

"OK. You can have the rest of my cake."

I smile and think, well, it's a start. Hopefully, someday they will learn to share.

## Ecclesiastes (Kohelet) 11:1,2

Cast your bread upon the waters,

For your gifts will return to you.

Distribute your portions among many,

For you cannot know what misfortune may occur.

## Job 1:21

And Job said:

"Naked came I from my mothers womb,

And naked shall I return there;

The lord has given,

And the lord has taken away;

Blessed be the name of the Lord

# Things to think about

1. Is it better to be generous or selfish?
2. Does your generosity with others inspire them to be generous to you?
3. Does selfishness breed more selfishness?
4. Is it natural for children to be selfish?
5. How do you teach them to be generous?
6. Do you feel good when you do something nice without expecting anything in return?
7. Do you do unto others as you would like to be done unto you?
8. Do you avoid doing unto others what you don't want done to you?
9. Do you believe that when you cast your bread upon the waters, it will return to you?
10. Do you "Pay it forward"? Do you do something nice and ask people to do something nice to other people in return?
11. Have you figured out a way to take your money with you when you go?
12. Do you give to charity?

# Things to write about

1. The times you were generous.
2. The times you were selfish.
3. In what ways do you expect your children to be generous?
4. What you have observed about generosity.

# Chapter 8

## Honesty Is the Best Policy

I am helping Rubin do his algebra homework. We stop for a snack. I turn on the television. They are playing a rerun of "I Love Lucy." We start laughing. Abbe Lane, a famous singer, is going to sing with Ricky Ricardo's band. Lucy wants to meet her. Ricky knows that she usually fouls things up and says no. Lucy puts on a fake mustache and dresses like a man. She tries to fool Ricky by saying that she is the substitute trombone player.

Rubin says, "Grandpa, why doesn't Lucy tell the truth?"

"That's the point," I tell him. "That's what makes it so funny. If she didn't try to fool Ricky, there would be no show."

"After she tells a lie, Ricky always knows the truth. Then she tells more lies to convince him that the first one was true."

I say, "I know. It's hard to keep a phony story going."

"She tries to be clever and outsmart Ricky," he says. "Then in the end everything comes tumbling down like a house of cards."

"Life is complicated enough. It is much simpler to tell the truth in the first place," I explain.

"If she was one of my friends, I wouldn't believe a word she says."

"I agree with you. I find that telling lies also puts a severe strain on my memory. And you know, my memory is not so good lately."

"What do you mean, Grandpa?

"I have to remember every detail of what I say to everyone. I can't tell something to one person and something entirely different to someone else. Sooner or later they will get together and compare notes."

He laughs and says, "Yeah, then you have to be like Lucy and make up a whole new story."

"I find that it saves a lot of time when you tell the truth. You also develop a reputation for honesty. People will believe what you say. I remember when I bought the apartment building on Canby Avenue in Reseda. We finished our negotiations and concluded the deal with a handshake. People know that my word is my bond."

"Is that really necessary?" he asks. "You can get them to sign a contract."

"I have signed a lot of contracts in my life. Some of them were worth less than the paper on which they were printed. A contract is only as good as the person who signs it."

"Why do you say that?"

"I've seen people sign a contract and still not do what they said they would do."

"No kidding? How can they get away with that?"

"The only thing you can do is take them to court."

"See, that's what I said. The judge will make them do it."

"No, in my experience, you spend a lot of money and you waste a lot of time. You get very aggravated. In the end they still don't do what they said they would do."

Rubin says, "I get the point. It is better to be honest and deal with other people who are honest."

He changes the subject. "You know Grandpa, last week a girl asked me how I liked her new dress. I didn't know what to say. I didn't really like it, but I didn't want to hurt her feelings. She looked like she was really happy with it."

"What did you do?"

"I told a little white lie. I said the color matches your eyes. I'm glad you like it."

"I'm very proud of you," I said. "You handled it perfectly. The Talmud tells us that we should avoid hurting other people's feelings. You don't need to be brutally honest all the time."

When the show is over, we go to the sporting goods store. I buy him some cleated shoes. He is trying out for the freshman football team at Fountain Valley High School. He wants to play wide receiver and strong safety. I hope he doesn't get hurt.

## Sir Walter Scott

Oh, what a tangled web we weave,
When first we practice to deceive.

## Things to think about

1. Do you sometimes lie?
2. Can you tell when someone is lying to you?
3. Is it sometimes fun to fool people with lies?
4. Do you notice a funny look on the other people's face when you tell him or her a lie?
5. Do you have to make up more lies to cover up the first one?
6. Do you have to remember what you told to every person to keep your stories straight?
7. Is it all right to lie to get what you want?
8. Is it quicker and easier to tell the truth?
9. Do you have a reputation for honesty?
10. Is it okay to tell a white lie to spare someone's feelings?
11. How is a white lie different from other lies?

## Things to write about

1. What lies have I told that I still can remember?
2. What lies have people told me that I still remember?
3. What have I learned about telling lies?
4. Where do I stand? Do I have a policy about telling lies?

**Roosevelt High School 1947**
Grandpa, first row, second from left.
Grandma, second row, second from left.

**Grandpa's brother, Stanley's first wedding in 1946.**
Bottom Row, left to right: Father Morris,
Mother Anna, Grandpa, Stanley, wife Ruth.

# 1948
## Doreen - 16
## Ron - 17

# Chapter 9

## Deal Fair In Business

I am helping Jeremie study. He is ten years old and his Bar Mitzvah is still three years away. He is already starting to learn Hebrew in his school at Temple B'nai Tzedek in Fountain Valley, California.

As we are taking a break, he tells me, "I am going to go into business when I grow up. I want to be rich like Bill Gates and make lots of money."

"How do you plan to do that?" I ask.

He replies, "I am going to start by beating Bill in a business deal. He is rich and can afford to lose some money. Business is like a game of football. Someone has to win and someone else has to lose. My friend Matt tells me that is the All-American way of doing things. All is fair in love and war."

I tell him, "You know, I have been studying the Talmud with Joel Grishaver. That is the study of Jewish laws and legends. There are many passages in it that deal with doing business." It tells us, "Don't put a stumbling block in front of the blind." In other words, don't take advantage of the other person's weakness or lack of information."

The ancient Rabbis who wrote the Talmud wanted us to find a way to do business so that everyone benefits. Their main concern was that we should always be honest and fair. The best business deal is one where everybody wins and no one loses. That is the original telling of the well known win-win principle."

Jeremie asks, "I know Grandpa, but why shouldn't I try to beat him fair and square?"

"If you beat Bill Gates in a business deal, he won't be happy with you. He won't want to do business with you again. As a matter of fact, he would probably tell all his friends not to do business with you either. The last thing in the world you need is to have the richest man in the world bad mouthing you.

"On the other hand, if you had a deal where you both benefited, he would want to be your customer. He would trust you and want to do business with you again. Not only that, he would probably recommend you to his friends. They could also become your customers. That is how a business grows by having satisfied customers."

Jeremie thinks for a while. Then he says, "I guess you are right, Grandpa. But you are a doctor. What do you know about business?"

I reply, "We all engage in some business deals during our life. In a broader sense, your daily encounters with people can be looked upon as business deals. You might want something from them or they may want something from you. You try to negotiate a deal that is fair to both of you."

"I don't quite understand what you mean by doing business where everyone benefits. Tell me about it," he asks.
After some thought, I say, "Let me tell you about the apartment building I bought from Andy Williams. I actually dealt with his father, who was one of the kindest gentlemen I ever met. The building was next door to one that I already owned. It was a good one and I wanted to buy it. I figured out what a fair price would be and made him an offer.

"The timing was fortunate for both of us. He evidently needed the money then. Andy was going to open up a theater in Branson, Missouri. He named it *Moon River*. It was tremendously successful. In fact, we saw it last year when we went to visit Uncle Harry in St. Louis. Unfortunately Andy was sick at the time with laryngitis and could not sing. So, we missed him.

"Getting back to the apartment building, Andy's father realized that he might possibly get more money for it if he put it on the market. But, that would be a lot more trouble and take a lot more time. I was a qualified buyer and he could make a quick sale. Besides that, he would save the sales commission by dealing directly with me, instead of going through a real estate agent. We made the deal. Papa Williams also came to me as a patient."

"I see," says Jeremie. "You got the apartment building you wanted at a fair price, and he got the money he needed to start a successful theater. That was a win-win situation."

## Hamlet Act I Sc. 3

Neither a borrower nor a lender be;
For loan oft loses both itself and friend,
And borrowing dulls the edge of husbandry.
This above all: To thine own self be true,
And it must follow, as the night the day,
Thou canst not be false to any man.
### Shakespeare

## Things to think about

1. Are business ethics different from everyday ethics?
2. Are your business associates friends or competitors?
3. Do you think that "all is fair in love and war"?
4. Is cheating so common in business that you feel you have to go along?
5. Can you be an honest person and a cheating businessman?
6. Can you completely atone by giving to charity?
7. How do you get repeat business if you cheat?
8. Do you feel good or bad when you fool someone else in order to win?
9. What do you think about applying the win-win principle to business?
10. Are everyday dealings with people sometimes like business transactions?
11. Do you believe in the *Godfather* ethic, with different values for business and family life?

## Things to write about

1. How have you conducted your business?
2. What do you recommend to your children about business?
3. Is success the most important thing in life?

# Chapter 10

## Be Kind to One Another

"You're stupid," says Ilana.

"No, you're stupid," says Jeremie.

I hear the words and frown.

I say, "You don't like it when somebody is mean to you. So why do you have to be mean to each other?"

"Oh Grandpa, we are just kidding," says Ilana.

"Yeah, we are just fooling around," Jeremie says in defense.

"I'd like it better if you found a different way to kid around," I tell them.

I think to myself, how can I get them to be kind to each other? The world can be tough enough. Their home needs to be a place where they can take comfort from one another. It is sad when they add to each other's burdens with cruel words.

Ilana says, "We were just talking. What harm can it do?"

"Talking can cause more pain than when you actually hit someone. Sometimes words can cause pain that will last an entire lifetime. Each time a person remembers those words, he or she feels the pain all over again."

"Jeremie knows I was kidding. Don't you, Jeremie?"

"Yeah, and so was I."

I think of something that Rabbi Schulweis said about saying cruel things.

"Let's say that you take a feather pillow and cut it open. What will happen?"

"Well, of course," says Ilana. "The feathers will fly out all over the place."

"It sounds like fun," says Jeremie. "We should try it."

"Now let's say you try to pick up all the feathers and put them back into the pillow," I continue.

"You'd never get them all back," says Ilana.

"Words are like feathers from the pillow. Once they are out of your mouth you can't take them back. People will hear and remember what you said. So, it is better not to say some things in the first place."

I look at them to see if they understand.

"Let's go get some ice cream," says Ilana.

"Let's go cut open a pillow," teases Jeremie.

I sigh. Maybe they will remember and be kinder to each other in the future. I might have to try again. Let's see. What other story can I tell them?

### Isaiah 11:6

And in that day,
The wolf shall dwell with the lamb,
And the leopard shall lie down with the kid.
The calf, the lion and the fatling together
And, a little child shall lead them.

## Things to think about

1. Are you always kind to others?

2. Is everyone always kind to you?

3. Are words more damaging than physical blows?

4. Is it hurtful when people kid each other and say nasty things as a joke?

5. Jokes usually poke fun at other people. Are they really funny?

6. Can you take back cruel things once you say them?

7. What cruel words have been said to you that you can't forget?

8. Have you forgiven people for what they have said but still can't forget the words?

9. When you are upset, should you count to ten before you talk?

10. Are you sensitive about some things that you wish people wouldn't talk about?


## Things to write about

1. Some of the mean things you have said that you would like to take back.

2. Some of the things people have said to you that you wish they hadn't said.

3. What can I say to convince others to be kind?

**1950-1952**

# Chapter 11
## Gossip Hurts

Ilana comes home from school. "My teacher is mean. She is really old and crabby. She yells at me all the time. The kids in the class hate her."

"What happened?" I say.

"She hates me. She gets mad at everybody all the time. Just because I handed my paper in a little late, she yelled at me. She marked it down from an A to a B."

"Maybe she is trying to teach you to get your work done on time. She sounds like a pretty good teacher to me."

She is still upset. "You know what else, Grandpa?"

"No, what else?"

"Rebecca wouldn't play with me today. She acts funny. Her parents argue all the time. I think they are going to get a divorce."

I say, "You know, Ilana, when you talk about other people and say bad things about them, it is called gossip. It is not nice to gossip."

"All of my friends gossip."

I say, "Then they probably gossip about you behind your back."

"Oh yeah!" she says, "I never thought of that."

I tell her, "My aunt Sadie used to say that if you can't say something nice about somebody, don't say anything. Now, can you say something nice about Rebecca?"

"Well, she is my friend and she is pretty."

"That's better."

"Don't grown-ups gossip?" She asks.

"As a matter of fact they do. Some people like to get together and gossip all the time. They like to talk about other people behind their backs. It makes them feel like they are better than the people they talk about."

"Does it work?" she asks.

"No it doesn't. When you tear someone else down, you're not helping him, and you're no better than you were before."

"What should I do?"

"I think it's better to brag about your friends and be proud of them. You can share in their accomplishments and bask in their glory. You can think about their good qualities. In that way you can become a better person."

"When Dad takes me shopping, I see gossip magazines in the checkout line. Dad says not to bother with them."

"Your Dad is very smart," I say. "Reading them is a waste of time. The stars and celebrities have their problems, just like everyone else. Unfortunately, people love to read the bad things written about them. Sometimes they even make up things that are not true just to sell more magazines and make more money."

"That's not fair," she says.

I continue, "The Talmud tells us that when you slander a person and say bad things about him or her, it is worse than murder. You are taking away that person's good name, which is the most valuable thing she has."

"OK Grandpa, I'll try not to say anything bad about anybody any more. What can I do if someone starts to tell me some gossip?"

"I like to change the subject. If that doesn't work, I walk away. That's the best way to let that person know that I don't like gossip."

"Boy, am I glad we talked about this. I don't want to hurt anybody, especially my friends and teachers."

Rebecca appears at the front door. "Oh boy!" she says, "I gotta go." She changes her clothes to go out and play.

### Othello Act III Scene III

Who steals my purse, steals trash....

But, he that filches from me my good name

Robs me of that,

Which not enriches him,

And makes me poor, Indeed

**Shakespeare**

## Things to think about

1. Is it fun to talk about other people behind their backs?

2. Do you like it when people talk about you behind your back?

3. Are the things people talk about true? Could they be exaggerating?

4. If people talk to you about others are they just as likely to talk to others about you?

5. Are there things people are sensitive about and wish other people would not discuss?

6. Does it make you feel better when you tear someone else down?

7. Would you like for another person to find out what you said about him?

8. Do you think that the other person will never find out what you said about her?

9. Do you think you shouldn't talk about others unless you say something nice about them?

## Things to write about

1. The mean things I have said about people.

2. The things that have been said about me?

3. What wisdom can I impart about the evil of gossip.

# Chapter 12
## Secrets Aren't Worth Keeping

Shifra gets dressed to go out.

Rubin sees her and wants to have some fun. He says, I know something you don't know."

"What is it?" she asks.

Rubin knows he's got her hooked. "I'm not going to tell you."

"Then, I'm leaving," she says annoyed.

Rubin keeps it going. He says, "It's about you."

"I'm going to tell Mommy."

At this point Jeremie is curious and comes in the room to see what's going on. Rubin whispers something in his ear. They both look at Shifra and laugh.

Shifra yells, "That's not fair."

Grandma and Ilana hear the noise and walk in. Shifra tells Grandma what has happened.

Grandma says, "It's not nice to keep secrets."

Rubin realizes that he is in trouble. He tries to put a favorable spin on the story and says, "I didn't want to hurt her feelings, so I didn't want to tell her."

"You'll have to find a way to tell her and not hurt her feelings."

Rubin gives in. "It's just that her socks don't match."

Grandma remarks, "See that wasn't so bad after all. Keeping a secret is not worth the effort. It usually gets around to the other person anyway."

Shifra responds, "I know. When I tell Sarah something, she tells everyone." She pauses and then says, "I have another problem about what you said. Yesterday Joseph told me a secret. It was something bad about Shannon. What should I do?"

"The best thing to do is to figure out a way to tell Shannon without making her feel bad," Grandma explains.

Shifra looks puzzled. "How can I do that?"

"Tell her in the most gentle way you can. She may be hurt a little at first, but she will be hurt a lot more if you continue keeping it a secret."

"I think you're right. I remember when I didn't tell Sarah something that Megan said, she got real mad at me for not telling her."

Grandma replies, "In addition to that, when I try to keep a secret, I find that it puts a severe strain on my memory, and my memory isn't that good."

"That's what Grandpa always says," Jeremie adds.

"Yes, it's true. I have to keep track of what I told to one person and didn't tell to someone else. Life is too complicated for that."

Jeremie says, "Secrets don't sound so serious."

"The big problem is that secrets are meant to hurt people by leaving them out," Grandma says. The other person feels bad because he or she is excluded. It is much better to include everybody. You would feel bad if you were the one who was left out."

Rubin is still moping. He wants to redeem himself. "That still doesn't sound so bad," he says.

"I remember a famous politician who did something wrong. He tried to keep it secret. He didn't want anybody to know about it. Unfortunately for him, the newspapers found out and published the story."

"Then, did he admit what he did?" Shifra asks.

"No, he kept denying the story, even though everyone knew it was true."

"I'll bet he would have been better off if he had admitted that he was wrong right away and said that he was sorry."

Grandma agrees, "I think so, too. So please don't ask me to keep any secrets. They end up hurting people and they don't serve any useful purpose."

Rubin gives Shifra a hug and a kiss. "I'm sorry Shifra. I didn't mean to hurt you."

It was a warm, loving gesture that made everyone in the room feel happy.

## Psalms 44:21
Shall not God search this out?
For he knoweth the secrets of the heart.

## Things to think about

1. Are secrets harmless?
2. Does knowing a secret about another person give you power over him or her?
3. Does having a secret make you better than someone else?
4. Does anything ever stay secret?
5. How do you feel when others keep secrets about you?
6. Do you have to lie and make up stories to keep secrets?
7. How many politicians can you remember who got caught up in their secrets?
8. Do political cover stories work or do they backfire?
9. Do you trust people who tell you secrets about others?
10. Is it hard to keep track of the secrets you have told? Does it strain your memory?

## Things to write about

1. What secrets did I tell that I wish I hadn't revealed?
2. What secrets did others tell me that I wish they hadn't?
3. Some of the secrets that politicians have tried to keep.

# Grandpa's Grandchildren

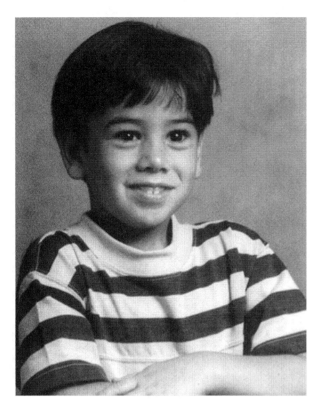

**Rubin at age 6**

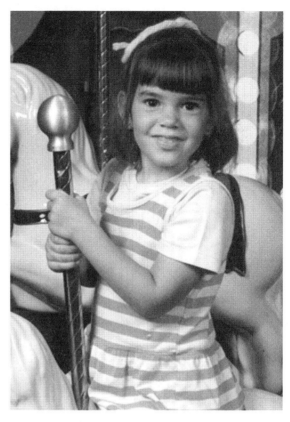

**Shifra at age 4**

**Ilana at age 6**

**Jeremie at age 5**

# Grandma and Grandpa's 50th Wedding Anniversary Party - 2002

Grandma and Grandpa singing and dancing.

Grandma and Grandpa's grandchildren and nephews.

# Chapter 13

# Are We The Chosen People?

Shifra comes home from Sunday school with a puzzled look on her face. She asks, "Grandpa, our teacher says that the Jews are God's Chosen People. What does he mean?"

I tell her, "I don't like that saying. It embarrasses me. It makes us sound like we consider ourselves to be better than other people. I don't think that Jews feel that way. I know that I don't.

I will give you the historical answer. God started with Adam and Eve. Within a few generations, people became so corrupt that He decided to destroy them with a flood. He started all over again with Noah and his family. That didn't work out either. People began to misbehave in a very short time. So, He decided to create a people who would become a good example to the other nations of the world. That's when He chose us."

She says, "In that sense, being chosen is not such a big honor. It carries a big responsibility."

I say, "You are right. Remember Tevye in the play "Fiddler on the Roof"? He was constantly complaining to God about his *tzuris,* which is the Yiddish word for problems."

Tevye said, "God, why did you have to choose us? Why don't you give the honor to someone else for a change?"

She thinks of another question, "How can we be an example? There are so few of us. Our teacher told us that there are only twenty million Jews in the whole world. Even in the United States we are only six million out of a population of three hundred million. That is only two percent."

I explain, "Size makes no difference. Look at Israel. It's a tiny country, no bigger than the state of Vermont. It has a total population of only six million, yet it's constantly in the news. She is widely criticized for moral lapses, that are excused and even taken for granted by other countries.

At this time, terrorists are active everyday in Israel. They try to kill children and innocent civilians by blowing themselves up in stores and busses. Recently, these stories are sometimes buried toward the back pages of the newspaper. Whenever Israel retaliates, the story makes headlines all over the world. Everyone condemns her. She is held to a higher standard."

I continue, "It makes no difference whether we agree or disagree about the chosen people issue. The phrase has stuck. The world looks to us, and we consider ourselves to be God's Chosen People. We have to try to do the right thing all the time."

Shifra looks puzzled. "I don't always know what is the right thing. Everybody has a different opinion. Sarah wants me to do one thing and Rebecca wants me to do something else. I feel like the rope in a game of tug-of-war. What am I to do?"

I laugh because I have been that same rope many times in my life. I say, "Sometimes you have to think very hard to figure it out. The solution may not be obvious. It may not be the first or second thing that comes to mind. Sometimes you have to mull it over for a while. The solution will usually come to us, sometimes in the middle of the night. You wake up and say, 'Aha that is it.'"

"I know, that has already happened to me a few times."

"When we know what is right, we can't take the easy way out. What we do matters. We are connected to four thousand years of Jewish history. Our life has a purpose."

I tell her, "When I was your age there was a lot of anti-Semitism in this country."

"I never knew that. No one has ever bothered me," she says.

"I know, and I am very thankful for that. Nowadays we are accepted and even admired. We have a lot more choices in our lives. We can even choose not to be Jewish. Some of our people are choosing to assimilate. It's a pity. They don't know what they are missing. All they really need to do is study and learn more about Judaism. If they did, I'm sure they would want to remain as one of the chosen people."

## Isaiah 42:6

I, The Lord, have called you in righteousness,
And will hold your hand.
I will keep you and give you
As a covenant people
As a light to the nations.

## Things to think about

1. Do you think the Jews are God's chosen people?
2. Does it make them better than other people?
3. Can you think of ways, other than using a chosen people, for God to encourage people to behave better?
4. Is it a blessing or a curse to be chosen?
5. How does it make all of the non-chosen people feel?
6. Do all Jews behave like they are the chosen people?
7. Can non-Jews be an example to others?
8. Does being chosen encourage all Jews to act better?
9. Will the day come when everybody in the world behaves like chosen people?


## Things to write about

1. When have I acted like one of the chosen people?
2. When have I not?
3. How can I use "chosenness" to become a better person?

# Chapter 14

# We Don't Need To Swear

We are baby-sitting our grandchildren one afternoon. We are watching a movie on television. A man says to a woman, "You are a *bleep, bleep, bleep.*" The woman replies, "Why don't you *bleep, bleep, bleep*?"

I say, "Let's go to the Megaplex Theater and see a family movie?"

While we were standing in line a man is talking loudly behind us. Every other word is *bleep* this and *bleep* that. I start to turn around to remind him that there are children present, but we are already at the ticket window.

The movie is rated PG13. The actors and actresses are cute adolescents who talk about *bleep* and *bleep.*

Afterwards we stop to have ice cream. I say, "I don't think they need to have all of that swearing in the movies."

"Don't be so square," says Rubin. "You hear the same thing on television all the time. You wouldn't want to hear the words in the songs we listen to."

I respond, "It's done to make more money. They know that kids will hear the dirty words and tell their friends, who will then want to see the movie or listen to the song."

"Some of my friends are using swear words," Shifra says.

"You don't have to be like them," I tell her. I'll have to admit that I did some swearing myself when I was younger when I was out with the boys. It was a fun thing to do at the time. We were just showing off. But now I know better. I don't like to swear. It just doesn't feel right to me."

Shifra says, "People don't seem to mind."

I reply, "Maybe they do mind and maybe they don't. Some people are offended, but they may not say anything. As a matter of fact, I usually take the easy way out and don't make a fuss when I hear other people cuss."

Rubin says, "Sometimes I feel like cussing to express myself."

I say, "You don't have to use swear words. You have a large vocabulary and can express yourself without them. People who swear are seen as coarse and uneducated."

He says, "You're right. I think the same thing when I see others swearing."

I say, "Other people will look at you and wonder what kind of family you come from. It reflects back on us. So, I would appreciate it, if you didn't swear.

"OK Gramps, we won't."

## Romeo and Juliet Act II, Sc.1

What's in a name?

That which we call a rose.

By any other name,

Would smell as sweet.

**Shakespeare**

## Things to think about

1. Do you like to swear sometimes?
2. How do you feel when you hear others around you swear?
3. What do you think about the person who swears?
4. Does it lower your value when you swear in public?
5. Is it fun to listen to swear words in the movies or in songs?
6. Are there times and places to swear and other times when it is not appropriate?
7. Does swearing show a lack of vocabulary?
8. Can you learn to express yourself without swearing?
9. Do you ask other people not to swear around you or do you just let it go?

## Things to write about

1. What are my own habits regarding swearing?
2. What I think when I hear others swear.
3. What advice can I give about swearing?

**50th Wedding Anniversary Portrait**

# Ethical Will Worksheet

**Ethical Will of** _____
(Write your name)

Dear_____,_____,_____,_____
(Write the names of the recipients of your will)

I love you. My greatest wish is that you love one another and that you will always be together in body and in spirit. Rally together in times of trouble.

My _____heritage has been important to me. I
(Religion or Organization)

hope it will be important to you.

These are the moral values by which I have tried to guide my life. They will be important long after your money and material possessions have turned to dust.


1. Honesty _____

2. Kindness _____

3. Fairness in life and business _____

4. Sharing _____

5._____

6._____

7._____

8._____

9._____

## My Special Hopes For You:

1._____

2._____

3._____

4._____

5._____

6._____

7._____

8._____

9._____

## Personal Messages:

1._____

2._____

3._____

4._____

5._____

6._____

7._____

8._____

9._____

### I will be with you forever,

**Love,**_____

(Sign your name)

# Bibliography

**Ethical Wills-Putting Your Values on Paper**
Barry k. Baines, M.D. Perseus Publishing
The most complete guide on how to write your own Ethical Will. If you read only one other book, this is the one.

**So That Your Values Live On – Ethical Wills and How to Prepare Them**
Jack Riemer and Nathaniel Stampfer, Jewish Lights Publishing
The ultimate authority on the subject. Excellent examples of ethical wills throughout the ages.

**This I Believe - Documents of American Jewish Life**
Jacob Rader Marcus, Jason Aronson, Inc.
Ninety-one ethical wills dating from 1706. It describes the people who wrote the ethical wills before you read them. Every one is a gem.

**Hebrew Ethical Wills**
Israel Abrams, Jewish Publication Society
Originally published in 1926 as two volumes. It contains examples of ethical wills dating back to the Bible. For those who want extensive examples of ethical wills.

**Aging Well**
George E. Vaillant, M.D., Little Brown and Company
Advise based on a fifty year Harvard medical study.

**From Age-ing to Sage-ing**
Zalman Schacther-Shalomi and Ronald S. Miller
Warner Books
Excellent advice on how to age gracefully.

# Thank you for reading my book.
# Why not recommend it to a friend?

## Quick Order Form

**Ship to**: **(Please print)**

Name _____

Address _____

City, State, Zip _____


| | | |
|---|---|---|
| _____Copies | $13.95 each | $_____ |
| Postage and handling | $ 3.95 per book | $_____ |
| California residents add tax | $ 1.15 per book | $_____ |
| Total amount enclosed | | $_____ |


To:  Ron Lever
17350 Margate Street
Encino, California 91316-2545

Phone        (818)789-0832
Toll Free    (866)789-0832
Fax          (818)788-1229
e-mail       Ron@AnEthicalWill.com
Web Page     www.AnEthicalWill.com

## About The Author

Ronnie Lever was born in St. Louis in 1930 during The Great Depression. In his early years he lived with his grandparents, aunts, uncles and cousins.

His family moved to Denver and to San Diego when he was six. His parents went to Los Angeles in 1937 to work in the garment industry. They lived in Boyle Heights, in East Los Angeles. Before World War II, they bought a house in City Terrace. He went to Roosevelt High School and UCLA. He married his high school sweetheart, Doreen. They moved to San Francisco where he attended medical school at the University of California and she became a teacher.

Ronnie then became Doctor Lever. He trained at L. A. County Hospital. He became Daddy after the birth of Karen and Rick. He practiced medicine for 30 years as a Urologist in the San Fernando Valley, where he published *Doctor Lever's Newsletter*. He is Uncle Ronnie to his nieces and nephews. He became Grandpa after the birth of his grandchildren. His friends know him as Ron.

After retirement in 1993, he has been so busy he doesn't know how he ever had time to practice medicine. He wrote his ethical will so his children and grandchildren will know what he thinks is important.

# Biographical Sketch

## Place of Residence

St. Louis, Missouri_____ October 3, 1930-1936
Denver, Colorado _____ 1936
San Diego, California _____ 1936-1937
Los Angeles, California_____ 1937-Present

## Education

Chula Vista One Room Schoolhouse_____ 1936
Wabash Avenue Grammar School _____ 1937-1940
City Terrace Elementary School _____ 1940-1942
Wilson Junior High School _____ 1942-1945
Roosevelt High School_____ 1945-1948
U.C.L.A. _____ 1948-1952
University of California School of Medicine_____ 1952-1956

## Post Graduate Education

Internship - L. A. County Hospital _____ 1957
Surgery Residency - Veterans Hospital_____ 1958
Urology Residency - L. A. County Hospital _____1960-63

## Military Service

Seymour Johnson Air Force Base_____ 1960
    Captain and Chief of Surgery

## Professional Career

Private Practice San Fernando Valley _____ 1963-1993
    American Board of Urology
    American College of Surgeons
    Associate Clinical Professor of Urology, U.S.C.
    Los Angeles County Medical Association
    California Medical Association
    American Medical Association
    Phi Delta Epsilon Fraternity (President 1972-1973)

Publisher - Dr. Lever's Newsletter_____ 1983-1993

Continuing Medical Education
    Training in Endourology _____ 1984
    Laser Training _____ 1985
    Lithotripter Training, U.C.L.A. _____ 1987